Haunting the Dead

Haunting the Dead

HAUNTING THE DEAD

Beth Ann Hooper

TOWER
of
BABEL

Haunting the Dead © 2026 Beth Ann Hooper

ISBN paperback: 979-8-9912927-3-3
ISBN ebook: 979-8-9912927-4-0

Cover photo: iStockphoto.com / Wisky
Author portrait: Jimmy Gray Photography
Graphic design: Puntspatie, Amsterdam, the Netherlands

Video editing: Andries Wijnker
Sound engineering: Quintijn Verhoef
Musical score film festival version Poetry in Motion Picture: Djurre Adema
Film consulting: Ronald Voort
Webmaster: Marco Rump

Also by the same author:
The Roots That Clutch
Lot (Dutch version of The Roots That Clutch)

tobcp.com
therootsthatclutch.com
poetryinmotionpicture.com

For Elizabeth and Hannah

"Then deep from the earth you shall speak
From low in the dust your words shall come;
Your voice shall come from the ground like the voice of a ghost,
And your speech shall whisper out of the dust."

ISAIAH 29:4

TABLE OF CONTENTS

Poet and producer's note 13

Home 15

Poetry in Motion Picture 21

Greek chorus poems from *The Roots That Clutch* 27

Exile 37

Reckless Writing, or Youth 63

Acknowledgements 105

I have always believed there is a natural connection, or to be more succinct, a natural marriage between poetry and film. When I saw the German filmmaker Werner Herzog in Amsterdam in September of 2023, just before I moved back to the US, I got my confirmation.

Werner Herzog told film school students there that film should evoke the same emotion as poetry.

'Nuf said.

The poetry in the last section of this collection is from the early 1990s when as an emerging writer and poet, immortality felt within my grasp and the world was my oyster.

Little did we know, it was the beginning of the crumbling of everything we knew and were.

In my literature classes at university, they would have called it perspective elements.

In real life, the events and what they foreshadowed can only be recognized through the hindsight of history.

And finally, there are very few of us on this tiny planet of ours who have not experienced some kind of great loss these last few years.

Everywhere I travel, I hear it time and time again, especially from my compatriots who love to spill their entire hearts out to utter strangers.

And I'm glad you did.

The healing power of art is this: Art is Life's pushback on Death.

HOME

Something sinister lurks in the forest
So deeply dark, so thick its blackness
Beating
Throbbing
Scarlet letters and crimson tides
Do not go into the woods with him
He has his demons
And famous voices of the eloquent dead linger in the air
Accents not heard elsewhere in this land
Only present in newsreels of ancient days
Black and white or just barely color
But here they live
They speak
And you hear
Tip toe
Tip toe
Through the May tulips
Tap toe
Tap toe
Tap toe
Tap
Tap
Tap
Oh listen and you can hear
Plath and Poe
Bodies enwrapped in their twisted tango
Spinning and dipping
Through the living room
Down the hallway
Through the antechamber
Spin
Turn
Tap
Tap
Tap
Out the door and into the forest
Where the dead brown leaves

Crunch
Crunch
Crunch
Under the turning of their feet
Where the dead brown leaves
Crunch
Crunch
Crunch
Under the rolling of their backs
The red and orange and golden leaves dance downward from
    treetops
Sinister ministers, scarlet letters and crimson tides
Onto their heads
Their backs
Their legs
Twisted and entangled
Fluttering
Downward
Silently
Winter.

And we drive
Like lemmings
To the path of totality

And there are families, of course
But so many
Alone
Like morning traffic
Mourning traffic.

On our way to the darkening of the sun
When God winks at us
Or so we hope.

And a guitar sound comes on
Oh no, not that song
On the radio
An old familiar
Cliché
So cheesy, stop, not now
We were just starting to live again
Just starting to love again

While eyes moisten
And well up with tears
So much tearing has occurred the past few years
One of you should have been here
At least one

Just one
And the cesspool of grief bubbles up again
And teardrops rush over the edges of eyes
As we pass
Mountain streams
Bubbling up
From melting snow
And leaping over the edges of rocks and cliffs and precipices
Cascading down

And all the cars
Each and every one
Are suddenly filled with people

The quick and the dead.

POETRY IN MOTION PICTURE

Jerry Garcia died sometime around the time
I was in San Francisco.
Kurt Cobain had died some time before.
Both deaths untimely.

Yet, Garcia, fattened with hedonism
His organs weakened from years of drug abuse,
Died of a heart attack.
The baby boomers mourned his death and lamented
the loss and hailed him as one of the greats.
Great what? Parasite?

Kurt Cobain, our whole generation did not even have the time to
    become
Parasitic, only just enough time to self-implode
Dreams promised that never materialized,
shattered in the hands of hedonistic predecessors, our futures
snuffed out our grasps, at the expense of our parents' carnal desires
and need for sedation.
And at Haight Ashbury
The runaways sit in a row along the street in front
of McDonald's,
My generation's death row,
All seeking the solace of exile,
And instead finding the exclusion of pariahs and a more
pervasive solitude.

And I, knowing how close
I came to being one of them,
Saw, sitting on the ground,
Such much like Kurt Cobain
Long, blond hair
blue eyes
pleading
"Could you spare some change?"
He, seeing he had caught my eye
I did not respond but walked on feigning I had never seen him
but he was much quicker than I was
"Could you spare me a smile?"
And with that request, he ripped my heart from between my breasts.

youtu.be/BdBWv5OdSSs

Love
Once
And one of a kind
And you know it in the depths of your soul
Spanning East and West,
Inseparable
Deeper than the ocean
So vast and defiant
The dots of our exiled lives
Connected by airplanes.
Immaculate

The immeasurable is always misunderstood
In a world that only understands the measurable,
And yet,
It is only the Immeasurable,
Who may keep accounts.

All that remains is the most rudimentary of sounds:

Sultana without sultan is just an "a".

youtu.be/Uo9dfDxspag

Beware!
Beware!
Beware of what you have wished for

O you who turn the wheel and look windward
Even though Yahweh, God, Allah has already written your destiny
In the wrinkles and creases of your forehead

Now you have drawn the Hanged Man.
The Lord, God Almighty has grabbed you by the collar
And yanked you up to see His Face
Screaming, "You are MINE!" which echoes now against
    the mountains

And there you hang
suspending
pending
awaiting His next move.

Foolish girl, oh
Foolish, westerner, stop your whining
We can't stand the sound and you cannot fight it
Your life was never your own
From even before its beginning

Earth's axle creeks

Not because it wants to but because it must.

youtu.be/powAhkBcIBU

GREEK CHORUS POEMS FROM *THE ROOTS THAT CLUTCH*

Oh Mr. Eliot
Fear the hooded hordes swarming over endless plains
Oh Mr. Eliot
Fear the present decay in Eastern Europe

Oh Mr. Eliot
Fear the Amazons

But there it was

Unreal

Unreal

O Lord Thou pluckest me out

O Lord Thou pluckest

Gentile or Jew

LOUVAIN, BELGIUM, OCTOBER 13, 2006
LATER THAT AFTERNOON

O Lord Thou pluckest me out

O foolish girl!
Listen to your mothers well!
Trust their experience and be wary of the wrath to come!

O foolish girl
Playing chess with the gods again
On your own

Oh woe to you
Bold girl
Too brazen for your station

Woe to you
Be wary of the wrath to come when you
Like the physician and the poet
Play chess with the One and Only True God

Oh hear the cries of maternal lamentation
Oh hear the cries of woe

OOOOOHHHHH professor
What have you to fear from three little witches
When there were more Modernists to consider?

Oooohhh classicist
In your ivory tower so concentrated on Europe
When you should have looked West and also considered Williams

O woe to you, myopic man
Your student you underestimated has outperformed you
Innately.

No one can escape the roots that clutch.

Their tentacles are inescapable.

EXILE

then
there
at that moment in time
you were there
but now
vanished
your loss now
is so acute
but will diminish
with each rotation of the Earth
each completed orbit
turning constantly
spinning us all out of control

The Angel of Death has descended upon us

Wrapping his wings ever so snuggly
around the Earth
yet
Tightly enough
that we do not notice the hour of our death

suffocating our lungs
suffocating our souls
snuffing out the final atom of oxygen in our red blood cells
turning us blue
deathly blue
icy blue
and we hear down an opaque grapevine
of how those we loved
have vanished from our midst
disappearing acts
beyond any magician's imagination
rendering
life itself
as the illusionist's best act

yet

Green
It was green
just like the feeling
just like the feeling

Take it
Mom added water
to dilute the taste the medicine
Green
the pain was green
and the medicine, too
so terrible
Mom added water
to dilute the greeeeen
medicine taste
medicinal

Driving along
the river
churning
churning
my stomach
churning
She picked up the brown bottle
with the green medicine
We waited in the station wagon light blue
Ford
so hot the car
the summer
the sun shone through
the car window
the angle of the rays
shining on my arm diagonally
parked along the river
so brown
here take it
I've added a little water

but the taste lingers
malingers so greeeeeen
so medicinal
like the sticky brain things
that fall from the trees
and lie broken
along the road
churning
churning
the river
so wild
where's the other side?
how many have died
in the river's churning tide?

Green
Taste it.

Lying in bed
rubbing my scalp
(I was too young to know that word)
I see the light from the hallway
my finger hits a bump
it won't budge
calling Mom
A bump!
Mom, a bump on my head!
She comes and looks
tilts my head toward the nightlight
A tick!
You have a tick!
Where are the tweezers?
Then it was Rocky Mountain Fever
before Lyme took over.
One disease takes over another
from the same parasite.

living in a state of decomposition
rotting
before your own death
an emptiness
endless emptiness
time does not slip through your fingers like grains of sand
no
it is the melting of years into one another
the accumulation of tears
swelling
overwhelming
inundating
wondering what could have been
if you hadn't wandered so far

CHILDREN

The chorus
in the Greek tragedy of your life
witnessing everything
silently taking everything in
waiting to bombard you
with their flamethrowing scorn.

While moving
boxes of books
languages foreign
two corpses lie behind them
spiders
same species
two of a kind
who had fought to the death
entangled in each other's legs
interchanging colors
the struggle to live and survive
in a tempest of rage and territorial drift
amounted
to
nothing
but
death.

Upon visiting your house
all I find are testaments to me
scattered on the dining room table

the couch I had chickenpox on
that blistering summer of skin and lips bubbling up
the first time dad turned on the air conditioning… ever
after I had infected myself
by kissing my little sister who had it first
so jealous I was
for your affection.

My first article for the school newspaper
an interview with a man at dad's office
who had played in the colored leagues

pictures of my sixth birthday
you had gone out of your way to make sure my birthday
wasn't overshadowed by Christmas
no images of you in the pictures
just Grandma
Dad's mom

The interview in the local newspaper
after I had gone overseas the second time
this time behind the Iron Curtain
so curious my compatriots are about this Communism
my large picture in the graying newspaper image
But no mention of you who gave me the greenbacks to get there
And now I, ghostwriter for the high and mighty,
Awkward technocrats, I make sound like
Shakespeare and Churchill
Your sacrifice ghostwrote me.

A baby magpie sits on the park bench
A cat comes too close for comfort
And the baby magpie's parents screech and chatter in Kamikazi dives
To each other, to the baby, to the cat
The chick wanders off to hide
Too small to reach the nest
Wings still unsure
So eager it was to taste its newfound agency
And the immortality of youth.
Yet the parents still screech and chatter and dive
Though the hope of survival diminishes
And the skies darken with the gathering and cawing of crows
Not one ounce of hope will they relinquish, this family
Even in nature there can be miracles.

The hare sits quietly
And realizes…

Gliding
Ghost-like
Over nocturnal waters
River, fleuve, flowing
Gliding
Guided by a steady, unseen hand
Pushing the ripples onto the banks
And into the waves
Gliding.

For centuries there has been a need
For a crossing.

First people and goods and animals, necessity.
Now cars and bicycles and motorcycles.

Vehicles upon vehicle
Things that must move
Carried over
Floated over
For centuries.
A bridge simply will not do.
And yet, always a need for a crossing.

Come and nudge up beside me
My dear, while the crickets wake us
It is safe here
Bask in the sun on the cool, wet, dewy grass
Just as you bask in my love
And I will keep you warm
And let you milk me
Warm, wet and dewy
Gently or rough
To make sure you are fed
And then I will show you
How to act
And grow
And eat grass
And become
An ewe
Or
A ram
Of your own.
And it breaks my heart
Crushes my soul
The center of your universe
Must become negligible
For you to thrive.

The millstone
I cannot shake
I cannot shake
Shake like a Shaker
And it still won't drop
Never
Drop it will
Will
Never
Will
The wider expanse
River
River
Sea
Sea
See

Winter wanes
And the scent of honeysuckles oozes
From the hedge along the sidewalk.

The sun warms the earth
Slowly glowing
And the river's vast expanse quickens
Deepens

Come and play on the riverbanks
Come
Come and dance on the riverbanks
Dance
The river beckons you
Come

EXPERIMENT

I am the rat
Who
Boxed in
Smells the food
On the other side.
Just through that hole
My feet will skuttle
Just stick my nose through
That hole.
Got it.
This time
Mouth-watering
Delicious
Aroma
My tummy
Fills.
Now again
and again
but then
I've forgotten
One smell
My stomach
Gnarls
I must eat
But have
No hunger
Taste has vanished.
Feeling has dulled.
To a numbness called
Existence.
I am the rat.
I am the rat.

A restless nocturnal vigil
Tossed and turned
By teenage dreams
Soothed by the sound
Of a distant railroad voyager
Demanding its way in the dark night

A restless nocturnal vigil
Tossing and turning
The worries of middle age
Spurned on by teenage dreams
And then
The soothing sound of a muezzin
From my neighbor's clock
And the engines of a distant barge
Churning forward through the night

All will continue
Even amongst the ruins of a continent
Caught up in its own quicksand.

so
GO
Run
Run to Cappadocia
Like the earliest Christians
to hide
from
Christmas
Yes, hide from Christmas
with all its memories of pain and loss
and personal devastation
vast devastation
Hide, Christian
In a Muslim country
Hide
and seek

This river slithers through the landscape
Clapping the sides of the levie with a
Slap, slap, slap
Chop, chop, chop
Every time a barge grumbles by
And the grass bends and folds
While the winds whispers through it
The secrets the river holds
Sucked in its maelstroms
Feel its pull
Feel its pull
Tugging at you
Tugging at you

The dead are singing
Hear their voices pulling us hither
Pushing us forth.

The dead are singing
A call you do not even know you are heeding
The push and pull
Gravity
Inertia
The living
The quick asunder.

I always discover the rats
Just like I did as a kid
In Kentucky.
They never go away and always come back.
I saw them running in the closet behind the tv
No one believed me.
They never go away and always come back.
They found the rats
Because they found their babies
Under the dishwasher,
The truth always comes out in the children.

Icy and determined
You plow through life
Resolute as Judith opposite Holofernes.

Lanky and awkward
Extremities of your body lengthened too quickly
For your mind to adjust to
You languish in the injustices of adolescence.

RECKLESS WRITING, OR YOUTH

The assurance of a freight train
In the middle of the night.
Though we enter the irrationality of our dreams,
The empirical continues,
Though we sense it not.
The freight train assures us
That our nightmares
Are but an illusion,
And we can escape
Back and forth
Between worlds.

When it comes to our death
We go back to our birth
For before the face of death
We are but innocent children
Fearful of the unknown
Afraid of the darkness.

I'm feeding my plants.
I'm putting them in the sunshine.

I wish you were here.
I could curl up
Into the form of your warm body.
On the other hand
I'm glad you're not.

Damn
Another mosquito

Oh
It's a motorcycle in the distance

Maybe it's repetition that makes us prejudiced.

The title sounds familiar
That's because it's true
It's true.

A colleague said to me
My father used to say
I have a nice present for you
If you come at Christmas time.

The Magis' gifts
Given out of love
To the Child.

Children born,
Yes, us
Born to fulfill our parents' shortcomings

Nothing is sacred
Neither parenthood
Nor childhood

Irreversibly related,
Reversibly sacred.

Surrogate mothers
Sperm donors
Artists
Contracted to create.

The first time
A child was killed in war
Was the first time
The word sacred
Became obsolete.

The first time a child
Was hit,
The word sacred
Became abstract.

EPIPHANY

The brief moment
Our fingers entwined
The face behind them
The demonstration of the union
Of the two
The strength.

But within the mists
The water evaporates
And illusion and reality
Become evident.

Try and grab the wind
And it will crawl out
From under your arms
Follow it and loneliness
Becomes obsolete.

BOILING POINT

Open the faucet
The spout of my tea kettle
Catches the water
And my wrist bends
At the weight of the water
Sinking to the bottom.

Turn on the gas
Strike the match
Blue flames rise up

Set the kettle
On the flame
I must balance myself
In order to directly place
The kettle on the flame.

Straight ahead I stare at the kettle
Hands in my pockets
The water starts to rumble
More and more turbulently

Steam thrusts its way
Through the hole in the spout
The whistle screams through the silence
Hot tears stream from the edges of my eyes.

The urge to look at old pictures
From years ago.
Laugh at all those funny little things
You've forgotten
At night
I run
My finger
Along the curve of my palm to my wrist.

The shadow of a cat
Walks by my curtain smoothly
He places one paw
In front of the other
Only his shadow makes him
Noticeable.

The crack dividing
My two curtains
Is my weatherman.
The brightness of the light
Shining through
Tells me what I can wear.

Oh
Let me get a towel
I spilled the tea
Can I borrow your lighter?
Where did you go last night?
How was it?
Ok.
I ran into
Oh no!
No it was ok.
    was there.
Oh so you weren't alone.
No.
But still
It works on you.
Oh, sure.
You try not to look that way
Where   is standing.
Yeah really.
And you try to ignore it
But it's not easy…
Oh no.
SCREAM

Both heads turn toward the scream
Tea steaming from the mugs
SCREAM

Silence
Steam
Stand up and answer the scream.

Hello?
Hi! It's
Oh, hi!
How are you?
Ok. And you?

I'm alright.
Listen
I'm having tea with
Can I call you back?
Sure.
Ok. Talk to you later. Bye.

And hang up the scream
Crying baby demanding your attention
Intruder on warm steaming sugary tea.

Dandelion, dandelion
Where have you been?
Your white, white milk
From your stem does seep
White, white milk
Sticks to my feet
Over you barefoot
I run.

Buttercup, buttercup
Where have you been?
Your yellow, yellow petals
Do taste so sweet
Look how you grow
Around my feet
My bare, bare feet.

Tulip, tulip
Where have you been?
There you are
So black and blue
Inside I am frozen and stare
Straight inside deeper and deeper
There you are
Where you always were
Between the dandelions and the buttercups.

LATHER

The filth of an unstable mind
Smeared onto the offspring
Until the offspring gets a hold of soap.

There's frost on my window
But is it cold outside?

Clouds float past my window
But is the wind blowing?

The sky grows darker outside my window
But is the earth turning?

That sinking, sinking feeling
The sun and winter afternoon
Celestially embodied.

When the sun comes up
A new day to grasp hold of
A new star
Warming my window pane.

Green my plants
Blond my hair
Warm my skin

Warm my belly
Refreshen my throat
Fill me up

Wet my hair
Refresh my skin
Splash into my face

Shine on my skin
Shine on my hips
Shine on my skin

The blue darkness slithers and surrounds the space
Moonshine makes the black blue
The sleeper sinks into her own reality
Sucked into irrationality
The fear raises angst, anxiety
Grabs and its arm to stab
AAAAHHHHHHH!!!!

The freight train slowly continues its way
Through the black and blue night
The clamor of steel wheels on the tracks
Lays the sleeper's head back on her pillow.

Step by step
I stagger through the wavy dunes
The blond sands of your hair
To dive into your crystal blue irises.

We have a word called "beast"
And we have a standard upon which
We consider someone a "beast"
And we have a standard upon which
We consider the beasts "beasts".

Loss of lyrical STOP
Experience equals emotion STOP
Death of free naiveté STOP
Own your own Berlin Wall STOP.

Lone Survivors

Escapeés of the wild horses corral
Waiting to bite and poison the blood
Scar the arm
Redden the eyes
Dilate the pupils
Sizzle the brain
Numb
Nothing
No

(But we find other addictions)

Skies like a Magritte painting
Blond sands block my view
And oases iron out
My wrinkled forehead.

Sweet slivery slumber
Shines on your skin
Wish you were here
We could make golden sunshine together.

Suffocated desire
Silenced by fear
Longing for warmth
But cozy in the cold.
Confusion between past and present
Clouds the future.

so

So
the fabric of my soul
Still feels soft to a stranger's skin
So
Succumbed with gratitude
Hands shaken
Stirred with emotion
Someone else
Can
Wear
My hand
Sewn
Clothes
Too.

Your sulfurous stench
Rises to mind
And the darkness grows
A thicker black
From whose suffocating pressure
Emerges the worm
And whose singular bite
Hollows the fruit out completely
Leaving only shiny, shallow skin.

This arid isle
Death of life
Doomed with damnation and death
Because meticulous manners
Slowly suffocate the soul
Escapists flee
But origin is a rock bound to the ankle
Back to his funeral.

If I was death
I could live forever
But I'm not so
Don't expect too much from me.

I'm looking for a man
Who will
Masturbate with the ghosts of my mind
And sink into a spiritual well
Filled with waters as warm
As your mother's womb

So when I extend my hand
Who will grab it
Come my hands are as bloody as
Anyone else's
But some are bloodier
Than mine

In this Auschwitz called a civilized city
We float along the River Styx
After we've sailed solitarily
On the scummy River Rhine

But there's nothing left to feel
On the River Styx.

This arid isle
Saturated with fat from fish and chips
Clogging its heart with meticulous manners
Causing its poets to flee
But origin says
"Thank God I'm an Englishman."

Oh, oh baby fascist
You must learn to accept change
You can't always have blond neighbors
Oh, baby fascist
Stop blaming everyone else
You must grow up and accept the consequences
Of your actions.

This mist descends on Holland
Like a deadly blanket of snow
That will never fade
Hanging in limbo
Like an unemployed
Waiting for a job.

I'm looking for a man
Who'll masturbate w/
The ghosts of my mind
So that it won't seem
Like
He's masturbating w/ me.

There's an arid isle
In my soul
That no hurricane of love
Could saturate
But I want him to try
Again and again
Like
I try again and again
In the hope
That this island
Will become fertile again
And
Panthers will run under
Palm trees
And cockatoos will cackle
Overhead
And waterlilies will float
In the streams
And orchids will bloom at dawn.

But I won't tell him this.
His animal instincts
Will just have to tell him
Of my surreptitious isle
And he'll have to discover it
Before he starts his
Spurious
Sacerdotal
Masturbation.

What's there left to do
In a Europe
Full of Eichmanns
And Jews
And scapegoats
And concentration camps
And systematic death

What's there left to do
In a Europe
Full of skinheads
And immigrants
And scapegoats
And recurring
Hate
Hate
Hate

What's there left to do
In Europe
Other than make love?

And so
Angry children have given voice
To their rage
And their ever domineering father
Has told them
They have no reason to be angry
Because it's normal
Not to have a roof over your head
Or food on your plate
And to feel like an adult
On the day you were born.

There's a huge seed
That falls out of a huge tree up the road
We don't know what to call them
So we just call them green brains
Daddy says
They used to be red.
They just fall out of the tree
And lie on the street
We kick them until
They split apart
And white stuff oozes out of them
It sticks to our hands
Mom makes us wash our hands right away
They could be poisonous she says.

She put one in the cornucopia last Thanksgiving
We didn't have enough gourds.

Drab
Drizzle
Drenching
Drenching
Quenching
The throb of factories forgone
Beats still,
In the hearts of the men and women
Parading over the streets
A relief subsides
This is not London
Accents singing
Identifying
Their place on this arid isle.

ACKNOWLEDGEMENTS

Thank you, Kjeld de Ruyter, for your mesmerizing graphic design once again.

And thanks to my creative crew, Andries Wijnker, Djurre Adema, Quintijn Verhoef, Marco Rump and last but definitely not least Ronald Voort who have all stuck by me despite the ocean between us.

To fellow writer and good friend Phyllis Edgarly Ring and to my other good friend in New Hampshire, Kathy Jones, thank you for bringing me home.

To Masheri Chappalle, President of the New Hampshire Writers' Project, thank you for welcoming me into the fold of this writers' haunt we call New Hampshire.

To Keri-Rae Barnum, CEO of New Shelves Books, thank you for helping me navigate the book world here in the States and for your ingenious suggestions that helped shape this collection of poetry.

To all the staff at Bookery in Manchester, New Hampshire for your undying support of my work literally since I arrived.

To fellow poet Selami Sehsuvaroglu whose undying support and never-ending encouragement has sustained me for years.

And finally, I would like to thank someone whose name I no longer know. When I was a child in the first grade at Tates Creek Elementary School in Lexington, Kentucky, a poet came to speak to us that spring. There in the gym, he stood and took our questions while we sat cross-legged on the floor.

I raised my hand and asked him, "Can a poet write what he wants?"

He answered, "I've never ever been asked that question before in all the places I've visited!"

The children's ooohs and aaas immediately circulated through the immense space.

He proceeded to explain that a poet should sometimes watch his language. I'm sure he had to say this. I mean this was the South in the mid-1970s and he was speaking to six-year olds.

But, yes, he continued, if he wanted to, a poet could even use swear words.

And at the age of six, I had my confirmation.

Live free or die.